T0094680

TESTIFY

Testify

POEMS BY JOSEPH LEASE

COFFEE HOUSE PRESS

MINNEAPOLIS 2011

Coffee House Press books are available to the trade through our primary distributor, Consortium Book Sales & Distribution, www.cbsd.com or (800) 283-3572. For personal orders, catalogs, or other information, write to: info@coffeehousepress.org.

Coffee House Press is a nonprofit literary publishing house. Support from private foundations, corporate giving programs, government programs, and generous individuals helps make the publication of our books possible. We gratefully acknowledge their support in detail in the back of this book. To you and our many readers around the world, we send our thanks for your continuing support.

LIBRARY OF CONGRESS CATALOGING-IN-PUBLICATION DATA
Lease, Joseph.
Testify : poems / by Joseph Lease.
p. cm.
ISBN 978-1-56689-258-2 (alk. paper)
I. Title.
PS3562.E255T47 2011
811'.54—DC22
2010038008

Printed in the United States
1 3 5 7 9 8 6 4 2
FIRST EDITION | FIRST PRINTING

ACKNOWLEDGMENTS
Grateful acknowledgment is made to the editors of the journals in which these poems first appeared: *Carnet de Route:* "Vow"; *Colorado Review:* "Magic," "Night," "Winter Night"; *Denver Quarterly:* "Send My Roots Rain"; *Fence:* "Enjoy Your Symptom"; *New American Writing:* "Torn and Frayed," "Try"; *Talisman:* "Home Sweet Home"; *Volt:* "America." "Home Sweet Home," "Torn and Frayed," "Try," "Vow," and "Winter Night" appeared in the anthology *Exchange Values* (Otoliths, 2008), Tom Beckett, ed.; "Send My Roots Rain" appeared in the anthology *kari edwards: No Gender* (Litmus Press/Belladonna Books, 2009), Julian T. Brolaski, erika kaufman, and E. Tracy Grinnell, eds.; a recording of "America" was included in *PoetryPolitic* (PennSound); a recording of "America" was included in *TextSound*. The author wishes to thank California College of the Arts for making the writing of this book possible through the generous awarding of two faculty research grants.

NOTES
"America" — Prods and lures: Amiri Baraka, Michael Bérubé, Allen Ginsberg, Susan Howe, Julia Kristeva, Laura Mullen, Marilynne Robinson. "Torn and Frayed" — Prods and lures: Rae Armantrout, Donna de la Perrière, William Goyen, Evelyn Waugh.

FOR BENJAMIN

One

AMERICA

November 2004–
April 2008

AMERICA

AMERICA

Try saying *wren*.

It's midnight

in my body, 4 a.m. in my body, breading and olives and cherries. Wait, it's all rotten. How am I ever. Oh notebook. A clown explains the war. What start or color or kind of grace. I have to teach. I have to run, eat less junk. Oh CNN. What start or color. There's a fist of meat in my solar plexus and green light in my mouth and little chips of dream flake off my skin. Try saying *wren*. Try saying *mercy*.

Try anything.

AMERICA

the sin most insistently called abhorrent to God is the failure
of generosity, the neglect of widow and orphan, the oppression
of strangers and the poor, the defrauding of the laborer—

We're going back home to
night pushes through money

We're going back home to
every vote counts

AMERICA

"Give in."

NASDAQ +12.90. Dow close: 10,617.78.

Hey kids, big sexy corporation!

Don't be a quitter—

AMERICA

It's the end (of something), the name in the leaves, you were there with a glass of blue when my face split in half— voices you heard one night in one town, just beyond the strips of light—leaves on grass, leaves on grass, astonishing sky—

Morning smells like piss, it's the end of the word, and I never quite "believed" (enough), or just at the wrong moment—

AMERICA

If birds

    If

The sky

  Is the

    Sky

If birds

  Tangle

    Prayer

  I

    I'm

AMERICA

America says fight the bosses. America told Ada. You can speak. You can speak. A million years away, the algebra of need, addicted to the Dow, to the camera, to the sound of wind, the summer sky, the winter sky.

Oh I
Need you're so soft

Lavender
Sky

Sky like whiskey

AMERICA

Wake up, you're not the truth—

Want my

back porch, want my front porch, want my milkweed,
my willow tree, want a new body, want a new mouth,
Christmas tipsy, kiss, yes—

I want to live forever, why not, why

not admit it—

AMERICA

What we're talking about is nothing less than rescuing a democracy that is so polarized it is in danger of being paralyzed and pulverized. And this is and you are and we are: say we are the people: we are people, the people:

say democracy: say free and responsible government, say popular consent:

say a democracy so polarized, say polarized, say paralyzed:

say free and responsible government, say informed public, say journalism, journalism, journalism—

AMERICA

Airbrushed

Gwyneth at

the Renoir

Hotel

St. Pauli

Girl

California Check

Cashing

Leaves and

Shadows

City of God

AMERICA

as if

there were no rules and dreams were safe—

write to your congressional representative,

write to your congressional representative,

write to, keep imagining—and you can't

get to the real world, they keep showing

the real world on TV

AMERICA

And—as if this phrase had never been abused in our life-times—to the ideal of a free society. It's midnight in my body, 4 a.m. in my body, breading and olives and cherries. Wait, it's all rotten. How am I ever. A clown explains the war. Oh notebook.

AMERICA

O Captain, my
Captain, citizen, citizen.

Feels like. You killed someone or no. You didn't. You did.
You're responsible, irresponsible. Didn't do it, can't remem-
ber. Feel like you might have. Might have. Killed someone.
Won't remember. Don't want to remember. Don't want to
be told again—

Try saying *wren*.
Try saying *mercy*.
Try anything.

AMERICA

If birds

    If

The sky

  Is the

    Sky

If birds

  Tangle

    Prayer

 I

  I'm

AMERICA

my scream is a brand name:

blue—for a while—

elm trees and summer and birch trees and sky, elm trees
and summer and birch trees and sky: expensive houses,
expensive houses dying: this lack of justice I acknowledge
mine—

America, one extra summer night—he wants to (you
know) feel like a giant eyeball—

AMERICA

You

Are past the boundary now, past the world that

Made the world, you are past the water's skin, past

The edge of coming home: you are free and you are

Drunk and guilty—like a picture in a glass, like the

Fullness of the sun, like a body come undone, you

Are past the water's skin, long and long and run

Away—

AMERICA

the sin most insistently called abhorrent to God is the failure
of generosity, the neglect of widow and orphan, the oppression
of strangers and the poor, the defrauding of the laborer—

We're going back home to
night pushes through money

We're going back home to every vote counts we're
changing the rules we're expecting disaster funding
the nightmare sure starve the poor try our new
prayer try our new blue Sunday try our new foot-
ball game turn off the shooting try our new
daydream and
try our

new rights

Two

TORN AND FRAYED

ENJOY YOUR SYMPTOM

Life is a series of shocks and injuries during which it is necessary to dress well, said Jack. I said, Why am I even walking these streets? That is a fart, said Jack. Really your whole stance of precious self-regard, your whole delicacy and force, is a fart at this point. No one cares. You're just one more sensitive ice cream cone in a world of unemployable spaniels. Then he stood on his chair and immediately five really handsome men and five really handsome women surrounded him. They chanted, "We will be your community. We will be your community." Really, Jack turned to me and whispered, really the thing you need is, you need a community; but you aren't going to get one because you're just another boring individualist. Puppies like you are a dime a dozen. You're so boring you should be on TV. The ten laughed. I said, I'll laugh at your jokes if you laugh at mine. You have no sense of humor, Jack said. You don't even know how to wear a shirt. You have to know how to sit in a chair and be outside the law. You have never known and you will never know. The next night I came back to the bar but I stayed in the shadows. Well, I'm afraid. Well, don't go outside. As soon as I go outside I'm in five different streets at once. This is wonderful: I can see five different views at once. I go back inside—nothing has changed: I realize there is only one direction I can go and that is forward. Just as I walk onstage, Jack, smirking like a game-show host, walks onstage holding giant quotation marks made of painted blue cardboard. He is saying, Folks, folks, stop me if you've heard this one before.

HOME SWEET HOME

Sky

Like whiskey and

Windows learn the

Sky

Sky like

Whiskey the

Sky and

Behind it

Lamplight

TORN AND FRAYED

I felt like winter, I felt like Jell-O—we lost the word *virtue,*
we lost the word *sister,* two hundred years of dark garden—
it happens so fast—believe me (I know you won't)—teeth
in coffee, dentures in piss—it happens so fast—might as
well, might as well let night in—

just laughing in a bus—

"You just want to die I mean capitalism just wants to kill
you I mean you just want and you just want—"

Bright

Branches

Your

Kisses

Your

Darkness

Your

Sky

You, you, you, you, you. Six when there's mist in the street, eight when your mouth starts to fade, nine when the drug starts to work, two when you hate yourself more. Three when you hate yourself more. Good old blank page. Slow down, green whisper, dry whiskers, ordinary twilight, ordinary, less hope. I wish I was Ezra Pound's towel. America, you can't be greed, America, you're only greed, America, one extra summer night—I wanted to (you know) feel like a giant eyeball—

"I tell you I was the stars. What do you care. I tell you I was a green pool on a summer night, heat driving everybody nuts. What do you care. I tell you just some more of this whiskey."

We

    Try to

Tell the

    Truth

And rain

And wrens

    And blue

Traces of snow in the

Rain

Deep

Autumn soft

Sung moons

Some image torn into strips, February morning. New Hampshire. Did you notice the bag on the dirt, did you notice—the golden retriever and no one is near—I was to be the dog. The faithful pup. And the dark was blue. And the blue was dark. We've all seen bodies before: contact all the fires of dawn, exaggerate, distort my angels: perhaps the big sister, steely and confident, perhaps the ordinary zombie, humdrum lost soul—

How

Shall I tell

You

How shall

I

Donna dreamt about Luke and when she told me she said I'm so glad I'm with you: great, thought I: my love is dreaming about her ex and I find that comforting: here's the joke—*These memories, which are my life—for we possess nothing certainly except the past—were always with me,* says Charles—

I can't remember anything—past the crust and down to the human, down to the want and want and want—

Your

Kisses
    Your

Darkness

Your
    Sky

You are

Strong very

Strong very

And words

And lost

And found

And blue

And

Green

NIGHT

"ready or not"—heard cold, heard blue night, saw moon,
branches—

"ready or not"—stillness and clear, bits of clear night, if the
story falls apart:

Miss USA gone wild, high school football, pro-business policy
solutions—

"solve your child's sleep problems"—

"ready or not"—you walked around like shame:

sparking and breaking—might give it back—might—

you're in the rain a million miles from rain and you and you
and you and you—

"ready or not"—blue town and summer and green town and
sky—

you're in the rain a million miles from rain and you and you
and you and you—

"ready or not"—I can pray in the shadow of the silo, in the snow, Chili's, Target, Payless, Wendy's, words washed in the shadow of the silo,

we bought you smoke over manufactured community; water, snow, and wheat—

"ready or not"—There's a dream in the rain.

A good dream.

They're running around.

They're in a play.

It's the shortest night of the year.

The light is light gray.

They're dancing around. Declaiming.

One saws the air.

One puts his foot on my neck.

It's a pretty light. The light is light gray.

I love what he's saying.

I want to show him how to do it. I look and I can't read the words. The words are tiny.

I don't have time to learn the words.

Is the holy place holy? Have you heard a naked yes, your own joy naked and far and near like another voice—

"ready or not"—And going for a walk on a night like this when the air is warm—the air is so soft—

"ready or not"—"When I was a child objectivity was considered an ideal in American journalism"—

"They have divided their nation into two classes: wolves and sheep":

"solve your child's sleep problems"—

VOW

Authentication failed. "Dignify my renaissance." In the rhythm of hair and sky, in this telling so rivers and ledges and horses, in this so hard then, so hard and free, in this telling cradled by slow moss, breathing September. I can't break again. I want to give you this. Wander all day, sleep like a dog, sleep like a wren, sleep like a fire. ("Your eyes are made of cash and going broke.") If I fall down or dance or go across the road where orange leaves are spinning in a thin gray rain. If I fall down or dance or go.

TRY

traces of snow, snow flying

    fast—

if anybody needs

    a branch in light—

don't

panic, let time wash you, you can swim—

the green hills turn to gray, gray turning

blue, just say *undershirt,* just say *hair,*

shoulders—I'm falling, I'm flying, I'm

waiting, I'm nothing, I'm

snow—

in the forest you can say anything:

O cream, a warm

night in December; your hips sing, dinner makes a

naughty dream—let's say I was Frank Sinatra's

toothpaste, let's say I lead a life of crime—O cream,

park your raspberries

on my moon—

if anybody needs

    the lake's glass skin—

traces of snow, snow flying

    fast—

if anybody needs

    a branch in light—

WINTER NIGHT

No.

Try again.

The illness (he thought he was "God") doesn't. No. Not Dostoevsky. Not a man in a blue coat. Not the illness. Not the demon. What I thought, what I. Not there. Not phrases. You can't. Worry. You can't win. If winter. If Franz Kline. If winter. If son or there was a something exploded. The consciousness. The finish. The simple. And wrecked the family called.

To you.

And love, love, to you.

Three

SEND MY ROOTS RAIN

presence was broken for a while, stillness was floating in plaid dark like a promise to the living and the dead, and the most horrible heartburn, and the old couple in the kitchen, lights out, lights out, waiting for sound—and the leaves roll just like faces, and the faces blow like thieves, and we all keep our explosions, and you taste joy in the night, and the lost boys answer slowly, and the corpse picks up the phone, and we all claim that we're holy, God won't leave our dreams alone—

Spin the wind,

Are

You winter—are you summer—here at

The end of the world—at the edge of the

World—every day—gets a little closer—

Moving faster than a rollercoaster—in

The night you kind

Of let go—and let it go—

I wanted to (you know) feel like a giant eyeball—under the trees, where nobody sees—I wanted to cultivate sky-blue emotions like a luminous village in the luminous dream of a luminous painter—sacred is as sacred does. So I watched the spider.

What could I.

What else. I watched it move.

I can't stand my own mind—

You just can't live through this—you're in the rain a million miles from rain, you started and started breaking and thinking and speaking and breaking—might give it back— might give back—swear you will—if you could only dream—the saddest dog I dream—then I'd no longer be in your eyes—

The secret blue lie—

(eyes shift

like promises, hair wet, apples and linen, just for today)—a
thunderstorm opens—birches in rain, are we breaking,
decorum slits my mouth, he finds a way to lie—lightning
and flat farms confuse me like wine—wine spills—thief,
thief of souls, thief, thief of light—fine, depression it is,
roast beef, Creature Features and Cheetos, Space Food
Sticks, thin birdsong, you your twin—"there was enough—
there was enough *alone* in you" *your eyes like rain eyes like
rain smile like rain* something about green torn silk:

"now"—you say take me to Heaven you

say take me to Heaven—

don't you want to say that—don't

you—

"now"

When the soul opens, there will be a cheap hotel: tender-
ness at the heart of the sky, the town, and not to hear any
misery in the sound of the wind—you came back to the
world: the green world, the fertile world, the corn world,
the gun world

You came back to the world and there was
nothing there

"polity breaks the church greets your faces

every sister against the glass glass wings

glass book glass snow glass secret story"

I believe

你你   you can do this

turn toward night, speak into it: the bright invisible red

blood: you want, you need, which is it—

something tawdry, he writes behind glass, on life, on death,

cast a cold eye—passersby pass by—

the eye, O priests, is on fire, the buried life, the buried life—

      shower door on grass, shower door on grass,

rain beads on jade—"you're it"—

Four

MAGIC

MAGIC

MAGIC

light on the balcony, start over—would she like to—oh

sweet dawn—you have a diner in your voice, maybe the

chamber of commerce—Oh sure, there's poison in him, but

he flies too, he really flies—

please

breathe my

newsprint

—my eyes don't fit—

MAGIC

everything's turning to gold, everything's turning to God,
everything's turning to dust

He became corners and toys, a feather. He became brides.

four minutes that could change you into mist
four minutes that could trade your soul for beer
four minutes that could dry you out like crack
four minutes that could dance like winter rain

MAGIC

spin and *sky* means

cash

(dancers

forget) and laughing glass cabinets, and toothpaste and

ravens, secrets and toilets, martinis and songs—*5% of the*

world's, 25% of the world's, population, resources, you know

all this, sure you do: minivan, Ativan, moon in my hands:

pigeons fight

MAGIC

sleeping

bodies—watch

them sleeping—

I

invented the family, private

property, and the state, I did

it,

            I laughed

          myself

          to death

       credit

     credit

        everywhere

MAGIC

maybe I should dream of nothing maybe that's it nothing
like a golden green angel like night sky oh the angel says
don't say like say nothing is a golden green angel nothing is
night sky nothing is dream

        snow

            blowing

        smell of

            wood smoke

        snow

            blows

MAGIC

branches, desire, little ifs of white spin in the bowl—

he wanted, wanted to leave—he tried and yes he tried any-
thing, the world is gone, the world is back—"I am not who
I am"—the sincerest form of commerce, I is a meaningless
dog, "I believe that"—

> lavender
> sky
> Dear
> Mr.
>
> Fantasy

MAGIC

Jesus told "me" so, he gave "me" laws, he gave "me" diamond
rings, he gave "me" laws, he gave "me" nations too—

                sure

                3:58

                a.m.:

      fog

          blue

NAFTA moves, money moves

MAGIC

Drinking

With a naked owl now,

Drinking blue snows, voices

Blue

Spank blue nighttown,

Green

Beyond the window's rose,

Where my eye just came

Untied—

MAGIC

your stormy stormy ghost green light torn dawn torn torn fire

your truck your grandpa burger deal City of God your business
business business week you city you City of God

So the new goth aftertaste

So the new goth aftertaste

A song

A senator

MAGIC

Jesus gave "me" laws, he gave "me" diamond rings, he gave

"me" laws, he gave "me" nations too—

"Water deal fails; prison plan OK'd"

Solve your child's sleep problems, fog, pro-

business policy solutions—

Please—

What is "the good life"—

Dear You,

MAGIC

pro-business policy solutions solve your child's sleep problems book-birds shining leaves hang fat grapes so mist deep kiss mouthful of wind like wet peonies his head is winter are you a worker health insurance health insurance health step into the water and step into the road step into the water and step into the sky health insurance greed health insurance greed before you know it you're lying in a pool of blood

I hear that everywhere I go

JOSEPH LEASE is the author of three critically acclaimed collections of poetry: *Broken World, Human Rights,* and *The Room.* His poems have also been featured on NPR and published in *The AGNI 30th Anniversary Poetry Anthology, VQR, Bay Poetics, Paris Review,* and elsewhere. Lease's poem "'Broken World' (For James Assatly)" appeared in *The Best American Poetry,* edited by Robert Creeley and David Lehman. Thomas Fink's book *A Different Sense of Power: Problems of Community in Late-Twentieth-Century U.S. Poetry* includes extensive critical analysis of Lease's poetry.

Originally from Chicago, Lease lives in Oakland, California, and chairs the MFA Program in Writing at California College of the Arts in San Francisco.

COLOPHON

Testify was designed at Coffee House Press, in the historic
Grain Belt Brewery's Bottling House near downtown Minneapolis.
The text is set in Caslon.

FUNDER ACKNOWLEDGMENTS

Coffee House Press is an independent nonprofit literary publisher. Our books
are made possible through the generous support of grants and gifts from many
foundations, corporate giving programs, state and federal support, and
through donations from individuals who believe in the transformational power
of literature. Coffee House Press receives major operating support from the
Bush Foundation, the McKnight Foundation, from Target, and from the
Minnesota State Arts Board, through an appropriation from the Minnesota
State Legislature and from the National Endowment for the Arts. We have
received project support from the National Endowment for the Arts, a federal
agency. Coffee House also receives support from: three anonymous donors;
Elmer L. and Eleanor J. Andersen Foundation; Allan Appel; Around Town
Literary Media Guides; Patricia Beithon; Bill Berkson; the James L. and Nancy
J. Bildner Foundation; the Patrick and Aimee Butler Family Foundation; the
Buuck Family Foundation; Dorsey & Whitney, LLP; Fredrikson & Byron, P.A.;
Sally French; Jennifer Haugh; Anselm Hollo and Jane Dalrymple-Hollo; Jeffrey
Hom; Stephen and Isabel Keating; the Kenneth Koch Literary Estate; the
Lenfestey Family Foundation; Ethan J. Litman; Mary McDermid; Sjur Midness
and Briar Andresen; the Rehael Fund of the Minneapolis Foundation; Deborah
Reynolds; Schwegman, Lundberg, Woessner, P.A.; John Sjoberg; David Smith;
Mary Strand and Tom Fraser; Jeffrey Sugerman; Patricia Tilton; the Archie D.
& Bertha H. Walker Foundation; Stu Wilson and Mel Barker; the Woessner
Freeman Family Foundation in memory of David Hilton; and many other gen-
erous individual donors.

This activity is made possible
in part by a grant from the
Minnesota State Arts Board,
through an appropriation by the
Minnesota State Legislature
and a grant from the National
Endowment for the Arts.

NATIONAL
ENDOWMENT
FOR THE ARTS

MINNESOTA
STATE ARTS BOARD

TARGET.

To you and our many readers across the country,
we send our thanks for your continuing support.

Good books are brewing at www.coffeehousepress.org